THE STRUGGLE
FOR MASTERY IN THE
FERTILE CRESCENT

THE STRUGGLE FOR MASTERY IN THE FERTILE CRESCENT

Fouad Ajami

HOOVER INSTITUTION PRESS
Stanford University   Stanford, California

www.hoover.org

Hoover Institution Press Publication No. 649

Hoover Institution at Leland Stanford Junior University, Stanford, California, 94305-6010

First printing 2014
21 20 19 18 17 16 15 14   9 8 7 6 5 4 3 2 1

Manufactured in the United States of America

The paper used in this publication meets the minimum requirements of the American National Standard for Information Sciences— Permanence of Paper for Printed Library Materials, ANSI/NISO Z39.48-1992. ♾

Cataloging-in-Publication Data is available from the Library of Congress.
ISBN 978-0-8179-1755-5 (pbk.: alk. paper)
ISBN 978-0-8179-1756-2 (epub)
ISBN 978-0-8179-1757-9 (mobi)
ISBN 978-0-8179-1758-6 (PDF)

*The Hoover Institution gratefully acknowledges
the following individuals and foundations
for their significant support of the*

HERBERT AND JANE DWIGHT WORKING GROUP
ON ISLAMISM AND THE INTERNATIONAL ORDER:

Herbert and Jane Dwight

Mr. and Mrs. Donald R. Beall

Stephen Bechtel Foundation

Lynde and Harry Bradley Foundation

Mr. and Mrs. Clayton W. Frye Jr.

Lakeside Foundation

CONTENTS

The Great Unraveling: The Remaking of the Middle East

IT'S A MANTRA, but it is also true: the Middle East is being unmade and remade. The autocracies that gave so many of these states the appearance of stability are gone, their dreaded rulers dispatched to prison or exile or cut down by young people who had yearned for the end of the despotisms. These autocracies were large prisons, and in 2011, a storm overtook that stagnant world. The spectacle wasn't pretty, but prison riots never are. In the Fertile Crescent, the work of the colonial cartographers—Gertrude Bell, Winston Churchill, and Georges Clemenceau—are in play as they have never been before. Arab nationalists were given to lamenting that they lived in nation-states "invented" by Western powers in the aftermath of the Great War. Now, a century later, with the ground burning in Lebanon, Syria, and Iraq and the religious sects at war, not even the most ardent nationalists can be sure that they can put in place anything better than the old order.

Men get used to the troubles they know, and the Greater Middle East seems fated for grief and breakdown. Outside powers approach it with dread; merciless political contenders have the run of it. There is swagger in Iran and a belief that the radical theocracy can bully its rivals into submission. There was a period when the United States provided a modicum of order in these Middle Eastern lands. But pleading fatigue, and financial scarcity at home, we have all but announced the end of that stewardship. We are poorer for that abdication, and the Middle East is thus left to the mercy of predators of every kind.

We asked a number of authors to give this spectacle of disorder their best try. We imposed no rules on them, as we were sure their essays would take us close to the sources of the malady.

FOUAD AJAMI
Senior Fellow, Hoover Institution—
Cochairman, Herbert and Jane Dwight Working Group
on Islamism and the International Order

CHARLES HILL
Distinguished Fellow of the Brady-Johnson Program
in Grand Strategy at Yale University;
Research Fellow, Hoover Institution—
Cochairman, Herbert and Jane Dwight Working Group
on Islamism and the International Order

The Struggle for Mastery in the Fertile Crescent

FOUAD AJAMI

I: THE PATRONS

Nowadays, the shadow of resourceful powers lies across the Fertile Crescent—the stretch of geography that runs from the Iranian border with Iraq to the Mediterranean. These are not the Western powers that enjoyed decades of primacy in the region. Iran, Turkey, and Saudi Arabia have stepped into the vacuum left by the retreat and disinterest of the West. Of the three powers, Iran must be reckoned to be the strongest. It has money to spread and plenty of bravado to impress the gullible, and its Shiite communities help paper over the Arab-Persian

1

divide and the differences of language and temperament. It is an outlaw power—its Quds Force, a unit of the Revolutionary Guard, can strike at will in the region, blurring the line between politics and terror. Its nuclear ambitions, and the scramble of the world's powers to contain those ambitions, give Iran great leverage in this regional contest. The suspicion arises that the theocracy's transgressions in this neighborhood can be forgiven so long as it is willing to halt its nuclear drive.

Turkey is an odd claimant to influence. A century ago, Turkey turned its back to the Arab domains it had governed for a good four centuries. Ottomanism was discarded as a new Turkish republic looked West, believing there was nothing of value in the old Ottoman provinces. But a neo-Ottomanist temptation was to rear its head with the rise of a younger generation of Islamists in the country's politics. The return to the Arab world was hesitant and rested on the preference of a fairly narrow political class. The bureaucratic and military elites and the Westernized intellectuals wanted nothing to do with this new calling. Still, what has been dubbed the "Sunnification of Turkish foreign policy" had plunged the Turkish state into Arab affairs. A daring leader, Recep Tayyip Erdogan, had succumbed to a grand Islamic ambition for himself and his country. His Arab detractors spoke of him as a new sultan and insisted that they were done with the age of sultans. But geography had its pull, and the disorder so near Turkish territory, in Syria, and Iraq gave the Turkish state new opportunities as it brought dangers aplenty.

In the scheme of things, the third of these powers, Saudi Arabia, is the most cautious of players. Saudis are supreme realists; they are immune to the call of great, risky endeavors. They guard their home turf but, for the most part, steer clear of the quarrels of others. They have wealth, and they rightly suspect that foreign entanglements will be a drain on them. But a new activism came to the Saudi realm of late. There were contests over Iraq, Syria, and Lebanon they could not ignore. A monarch who goes by the title of Custodian of the Two Holy Mosques could not avert his gaze from the Sunni-Shia fight at play in the Fertile Crescent. Iran, a rival in the Gulf, had pulled Saudi Arabia into this contest of nations and religious sects. Saudi Arabia shed its reticence out of a legitimate fear that Iran's bid for dominion had grown increasingly menacing. Saudi Arabia couldn't sit out the assault of Bashar al-Assad on a Sunni rebellion or the brazen conquest of Beirut by Hezbollah. In their modern history, the Saudis had an abiding faith in American power. The abdication by the Obama administration would, in time, force the Saudis to greater assertiveness than they had been known for. The House of Saud has great leeway over sovereign matters, but the rulers still have to be responsive to the *ulama* (religious scholars) and to laymen offended by the ordeal of Sunni communities in Iraq, Syria, and Lebanon.

The disorder of the Fertile Crescent—a magnet that draws outsiders—can be traced to the weakness of Sunni Islam in this region. In the Arabian Peninsula, Egypt, and North Africa, mainstream Sunni Islam is ascendant. The fault line that bedevils these lands is between secularists, who want to keep the faith at bay, and Islamists, who have stepped forth in recent decades to assert the hegemony of the sacred over the political. The Fertile Crescent presents a different landscape. Here, Sunni Islam was ascendant in the cities and centuries of Ottoman rule augmented Sunnism. Arab nationalism, too, had been a prop of Sunni primacy. But the edifice of Sunni power was fragile, and it would be toppled in the course of the second half of the past century. The military despotism of the Alawis in Damascus and the rise of the Shia in Beirut and Baghdad were a challenge that Sunnism felt as a great violation. When the rebellion came to Syria in 2011—the last of the rebellions of the Arab Spring—a terrible struggle lay in wait for the Syrians and their immediate neighbors. In Syria and Lebanon, the Sunnis, merchant communities, had to take up arms to correct for their military weakness. In Iraq, the Sunnis, suddenly powerless in the aftermath of an American war, fell into despondency only to be inspired by a Sunni rebellion across a meaningless Iraq-Syria frontier.

II: IN THE NAME OF THE SAINTS

"The destructive distortions of the tradition were all caused by men who had experienced something new which they tried almost instantaneously to overcome and resolve into something old," Hannah Arendt wrote in *Between Past and Future* (1968). The sectarian militias and the holy warriors battling across the Shia-Sunni divide bore out the wisdom of Arendt's insight. The world around them was new and distinctive, as were their feuds. That kind of novelty they could not understand or resolve. So they fell back on the past, borrowed its sanctity, and vowed to avenge its wounds. What is one to make of an Iraqi political man, Prime Minister Nuri al-Maliki, dividing the world between "Hussein's people," and "Yazid's people"? It was an unflattering line he drew—Hussein, the patron saint of the Shia faith, the Prophet Muhammad's grandson martyred in a seventh century battle in southern Iraq, versus Yazid, the cruel Umayyad ruler in Damascus who had struck with his whip the saintly man's severed head when it was presented him after the battle of Kerbala. These were old happenings, in the year 680, to be exact. Nuri Kamal al-Maliki, a political operative who had been formed in the Shia underground of Iraq, was making a bid for a third term as prime minister of his country. He had the resources of an oil-rich country at his disposal; he had managed to make himself useful to both Iran and the United States—presumed political rivals over Iraq. American Hellfire missiles and Apache helicopters were being delivered to him as he was doing battle in his country's largest province, the Anbar. The Sunni population of the Anbar had risen against his government, and he had done precious little to conciliate them. He assaulted their protest encampments and spoke to them in the conqueror's language. But he had virtue on his side as he belonged in the ranks of "Hussein's people." Imam Hussein had died on the plains of Kerbala, cut off from the waters of the Euphrates. He and a band of followers— seventy fighters, the sources say—had been abandoned by the Iraqis in the city of Kufa who had pleaded with him to leave his home in the Hijaz and to lead them in their struggle against the Syrians. Hussein had died a cruel and solitary death: he had been beheaded, his body trampled by horses. But now, many centuries later, he was being claimed and avenged, and the main body of the Islamic faith, the Sunnis, were being labeled Yazid's people.

And there was Imam Hussein's sister, Zeinab, buried in a shrine on the outskirts of Damascus. Zeinab had been revered and beloved by the faithful. She had been with her brother and his companions at Kerbala. It was she who presented Hussein's body to God, asked him to accept that sacrifice. She had, with her own body, protected Hussein's young son, pleaded with the soldiers to spare him. She had made the voyage from Kerbala to Damascus in shackles. The high birth—she was the prophet's grand-daughter—and the grief were vintage Shia themes. For centuries the shrine was the destination of believers—particularly women—who sought religious merit. But now the shrine had been politicized. Armed men from Iraq and Lebanon were making their way to Damascus. They came with a stirring slogan: Zeinab will not be shackled twice, they proclaimed, as they joined the fight on the side of Assad's dictatorship.

Out of the past, people in that particularly fractured part of the Arab world were attempting to make a future. In a once-lighthearted—almost frivolous—Beirut, warriors under the banners of Hezbollah were a veritable parody of the Iranian theocracy. Qom and Tehran were far away, possessed of an entirely different temperament and speaking a different language; yet, here were young men doing their best to imitate the trappings of the Iranian revolutionary regime. A mullah born in utter destitution, Hassan Nasrallah had ridden Iran's coattails to greed, power, and influence. He had become Lebanon's mightiest warlord. He made and unmade cabinets, promoted or sacked high army officers. His intelligence apparatus had the run of the country. A television station, Al Manar, carried his speeches and spread his legend as the "fighting Sayyed." Lebanese don't have to be particularly old to recall a country in which a man like Nasrallah would have been consigned to social and economic marginality. Those on the rise among the Shia were eager modernists, keen to assimilate the new ways of the city and slip undetected past Christian or Muslim Sunni gatekeepers. The world had been stood on its head; the Western embassies that once disposed the power in Beirut had been diminished. Nasrallah, with his black turban and *abaya* (cloak), had at his disposal a vast relief network: the needy looked to him, and his movement, for sustenance. There were skeptics aplenty among the Shia. But they were no match for what Iran made available to this satrap.

There came a time—in late April 2013—when Nasrallah himself owned up to his militia's direct role in the Syrian struggle. There was no need for dissimulation as scores of Hezbollah fighters had fallen in Syria, and a predecessor of Nasrallah's, Shaykh Subhi Tufayli, who had broken with the movement, had said he knew of more than 130 Hezbollah warriors who had been killed in Syria, sent there by the group's leaders.

"There are people who defend this area. Those people are working to prevent strife and are not the ones who are creating it. This is a very sensitive issue, given the fact that sectarian extremist groups have announced that if they reach the shrine, they will destroy it," Nasrallah said. "If such a crime were to take place, it will carry with it grave consequences. Countries supporting these groups will be held responsible were it to take place." The sectarian war was unmasked: the unnamed countries were the Sunni states in the Gulf, and Turkey.

III: BLOWBACK

The protection of the shrine of Zeinab was a convenient pretext. A more important military role of Hezbollah was its participation in a battle for the town of Qusayr in the hinterland of Homs, by the Lebanese border. Qusayr, a Sunni town, lay on the road between Damascus and the Syrian coast and between the coast and Hezbollah strongholds in the Bekaa Valley. The Syrian regime's forces had not been able to hold Qusayr, and Hezbollah had stepped into the breach. The claim that Hezbollah had ventured into Qusayr to protect Shia villagers was bogus. A battle for the Syrian coast had erupted, and the Sunni-Alawi city of Baniyas had come under assault. The regime's play was obvious: sectarian cleansing and pushing the Sunnis out of the region. The stakes for Hezbollah, both in Lebanon and the Arab world, had risen. Its forces had joined the battle to carve up an Alawi statelet should the regime conclude that the battle for Syria was lost. This intervention in Qusayr had stirred up the wrath of the Sunnis of Lebanon. A militant preacher in Sidon, Ahmad al-Assir was to declare the fight in Syria a jihad for his own community. Assir was the perfect nemesis for Nasrallah. The young man was a stirring orator delivering his sermons in colloquial Lebanese. He minced no words: Hezbollah was the Party of Iran, not the Party of God. In a speech in April 2013 (posted on YouTube of course), he described Nasrallah as a "war criminal" and said Hezbollah was more "accursed" than Israel. He taunted the Shia as accomplices of Israel who had showered the Israeli forces with rice and flowers when they invaded Lebanon in 1982. The cleric spoke of the distress of the Sunnis: they were being killed and belittled in their own country, and the forces of order in Lebanon, the army and the police, were instruments of Hezbollah, and the latter a cat's paw of Iran.

In the fashion of Hezbollah, but without the big guns and the vast crowds, the young men of Sidon gave Assir a role to play in this sectarian standoff. Sidon is the gateway to the Shia stronghold in the south. The coastal Sunni town of merchants, fishermen, artisans, and citrus growers did brisk business with Shia on their way to the villages in the hill country above Sidon. There was no love lost between the folks of Sidon and the Shia: proximity bred unease, and Sidon—once sure of itself, its urban ways, and the Arab nationalism that was the civic religion of "the street"—was in the way of a Shia juggernaut. The Shia peasants of old whose buses stopped in Sidon on the way to their impoverished villages from Beirut to buy the oranges and bananas of the coast had been transformed. There was Shia money, and Shia demography, and swagger, and a community touched by modernity. Hezbollah, and its allied movement Amal, dominated the politics of southern Lebanon, and Sidon had been overwhelmed.

Assir could not hold back the tide. He gave voice to Sunni resentment. The Sunnis of Syria being subjected to the assault of the dictatorship and to the forces of Hezbollah were brothers and kinsmen. Assir did not have the muscle and the money for this contest. (Rumors suggested that Qatar subsidized him and his mosque.) The Sunni political machine that held sway in Sidon belonged to the family of the tycoon Rafik Hariri and his son and political heir, Saad. But Saad had quit the country for Paris, certain that the assassins of Hezbollah and the Damascus regime would target him if he had remained on the scene. Assir had no kind words for Hariri. He railed against him as a coward who had abandoned the cause. Assir was an urban populist who fused religion and a sense of economic discontent. But the merchants of the Sidon souk could not adopt his militant way: they needed the business of the Shia, who could, when they saw fit, bring the life of the souk to a standstill.

The people of Sidon had hoped against hope that the Hezbollah political apparatus would stay out of the Syrian fight, if only out of a decent regard for the sectarian compact of Lebanon. But Nasrallah did not oblige. He was at once a political player in Lebanon, without doubt the country's mightiest warlord, and, by his own account, a soldier in the *wilayat al-faqih* (the Guardianship of the Jurisprudent) of the Iranian theocracy. The expectations that Hezbollah would "go Lebanese, go local" were in vain. Nasrallah had been here before. In 2006, the Iranian regime, diplomatically embattled and isolated over its nuclear program, sought a way out of its dilemma and gave Nasrallah the green light for a little war on the Lebanon-Israel frontier. Nasrallah had promised his political rivals in Lebanon a quiet summer, an opportunity for the traders and the hoteliers to have a good tourist season. But the orders from Tehran—to Nasrallah a religious obligation and the will of his financial backers—trumped the rules of the Lebanese game. It was then that Hezbollah struck, kidnapping two Israeli soldiers and igniting a war that went beyond what Nasrallah had bargained for.

Hezbollah fought Israel for 34 days, and this became Nasrallah's badge of honor. Fear, and group solidarity, reduced to silence the people of south Lebanon who suffered the consequences of that "victory." Never mind the death and ruin of that summer. Lebanese and other Arabs obliged, and Hezbollah's cleric, the "fighting

Sayyed," now became a cult figure. He was a hero in (Sunni) Damascus and in the streets of Lebanon. Less than two years after that terrible summer, Hezbollah would overrun West Beirut, the traditional haven of the Sunnis, and push into the Druze stronghold in the mountain. The arsenal that Iran had given Hezbollah had been justified as the legitimate arsenal of the "resistance" against Israel and the United States. But in May 2008, as the fighters overran West Beirut and put to flight a small contingent loyal to Saad Hariri, the Sunnis in Lebanon and beyond came face-to-face with the sordid reality of Hezbollah's power and with Iran's ambitions for the little "sister republic" by the Mediterranean.

IV: A WAR WITH NO SECRETS

The Hezbollah attack on Qusayr yielded a seventeen-minute video that put to shame the utterances of Hassan Nasrallah about the role of his militiamen in this war. The video is the work of an "Information Network in Qusayr" and posted by SAS News, an opposition outlet. It is mid-May 2013, and the video is a crude affair. Filmed at dusk, it is an unadorned rendition of a driver traveling a road littered with dead livestock. There is chaos on the road, and it is there for the driver to catch. There are families fleeing from Hezbollah, with boys on their motorbikes hauling their family possessions and the women and children in the back of open trucks. A woman with several children—too many, one would think, but this is a very young nation and the children are everywhere—get into the car. The children are crying, and the driver tries to reassure them that all is well. The mother is breathless. Unprompted, she invokes Allah and his mercy against the tormentors. Hezbollah is cursed as *Hizb al-Shaytan* (the Party of Satan). "They are celebrating our suffering," she says. "God willing, we will celebrate theirs." One of the children cries as the mother rails against the world.

"God is with us," the driver intones, who stops to talk to a woman by the side of the road. She wants him to film the wretched misery and the fear. Full of wrath—against Hezbollah and against the government that claims to hunt down terrorists but in reality kills women and children—she does not spare the opposition: they had forsaken the people and are interested only in money. "We don't want money; we just want them to stop this disaster." "This is the third day in the attack of the Party of Satan on the people west of the Orontes," the driver notes, turning the camera on himself. The narrator doesn't establish the direction of this caravan of grief; one would have to know the names of the hamlets, but it is the standard flight of unarmed men and women in search of safety. A woman dragging a cow behind her wants to record her objection to being filmed. "We have had it with filming our misery," she says. It is dark now, and the sounds in the background belong to the live-stock and the motorbikes. The driver tries to lend order to the chaos: he wants it established that this is an unprecedented attack on the vil-lages around Qusayr. These people, he says, are trying to join their kin.

The Shia narrative of lamentations has for-ever dwelled on the fate of Shia hounded by the mighty and the wicked. The woman and chil-dren in the car and the terrified villagers on the road asking for God's help must have traded places with Nasrallah: they were his victims, he was their heartless pursuer.

From the Qusayr Information Network, a fighter by the nom de guerre of Abu Ali, on May 20, sums up Qusayr's ordeal: "We are fighting Iran, Russia, the Party of Satan, and the regime. The whole world has left the innocent Syrian people on their own." By now Hezbollah was out of the shadows: the secret funerals of the fighters who died performing their jihadi duty were now public ceremonies. Hezbollah's "martyrs" were now celebrated as they were taken back to their villages. This was holy warfare with a twist: the fallen had their own Facebook pages, which displayed their pictures and the names of their hometowns. There were brazen distortions of these events. A Hezbollah stronghold, the town of Bint Jbeil, deep in the southern world, had its own website. The propaganda was heavy-handed: the Syrian rebels, one posting claimed, were fighting with Israeli weapons. That Syrian rebellion had to be demonized. Far be it for the town of Bint Jbeil to own up to a sectarian war. The people of Bint Jbeil, right by the border with Israel, had to garb this struggle in the familiar fight with Israel.

In this terrible struggle, there were no easy victories. So full of bravado, Hassan Nasrallah said the fight for Syria should not be fought on Lebanese soil. Naturally, his enemies did not oblige. Car bombs—the weapon of choice—hit Hezbollah's stronghold in southern Beirut in July, August, and November. The November attack was a double suicide bombing that targeted the Iranian Embassy, which was located in a Shia neighborhood. A motorcycle bombing was followed by the explosion of a four-wheel drive. At least 22 people were killed and more than 140 others injured. A Sunni jihadist group claimed responsibility and announced on Twitter that the attack was carried out by "two heroes of the Sunnis in Beirut." The jihad had come to Lebanon. The Dahieh (the southern suburbs of Beirut, the base of Hezbollah) would know no reprieve. Car bombs shattered its peace of mind and its economy. Hezbollah had radicalized the Sunnis, and the moderate Sunnis had been pushed aside. The Lebanese state had fallen into Hezbollah's hands. It was sheer fantasy to believe the Sunnis would be bullied into submission. There had been a time when the Shia commanded no military power in Lebanon; now, Nasrallah and his lieutenants had succumbed to the illusion that the Sunnis of Lebanon would remain uninterested in Syria's agony. The Sunnis of Beirut, Sidon, and Tripoli had wearied of Nasrallah's bravado. He had belittled them, and they were ready for the jihadists to avenge them. Predictably, in the aftermath of the embassy attack, Iran's ambassador to Lebanon said Israel was the culprit in this attack. But no one was fooled; the protagonists were caught up in a struggle of their own, with Israel a mere spectator to a bitter sectarian fight.

It didn't take long to identify the two suicide bombers who had struck the Iranian Embassy. Their biographies cast a floodlight on this moment. One was a young man of Sidon, the other a Palestinian from the refugee camps in south Lebanon. Both had gravitated to the network and mosque of Shaykh Ahmad al-Assir. The young man of Sidon, 23-year-old Moein Abu Dahr, was his city's first "suicidal." Not surprisingly, he was a child of poverty with a "complicated" family background, as the daily *An Nahar* reported on November 23. His parents were divorced, his father had two wives, his mother had remarried, and no one had bothered with his schooling. His father was a Sunni, but his mother was Shia. He had performed odd jobs when he could find them. In the fashion of young Lebanese without means, he had been a drifter. He had gone to Denmark, courtesy of a relative, and then to Sweden. Finding no opportunities there, he returned to Sidon and then made his way to Syria to join the fight. He returned once again to Sidon, as a *muhajir* (a voyager) in the Path of God, he said on his Facebook page. Three days before the attack on the embassy, he had called his parents from a cell phone in Syria to ask their forgiveness. When queried about his whereabouts, he said he was in Kuwait.

The second bomber, 26-year-old Adnan Mousa Mohammad, was one of six children. He worked as a mechanic in Sidon. Six months before the attack he had disappeared, and his family reported that he had gone missing to the authorities. After the attack, some family members said he had been "mentally unbalanced." Others closer to the truth said he was a religious young man of very few words, a secretive type. His family scrambled for cover, issuing a statement that they were innocent of his deed. They proclaimed their support for "the resistance" and for the Islamic Republic of Iran. *An Nahar* polled its readers on whether Lebanon had become fertile soil for a new wave of terror attacks. The results gave voice to the pessimism of an unsettled country: seventy-eight percent answered in the affirmative, seventeen percent went the other way. There was no shortage of thwarted young men eager to claim an exalted mission for themselves.

A tale from Sidon reported on May 22, 2013, in Beirut's English-language newspaper, the *Daily Star*, catches the sectarian antagonism whipped up by the battle for Qusayr. A Hezbollah fighter who had fallen in Qusayr was brought back to Sidon for burial. The young fighter, Saleh Sabbagh, came from a mixed background. His father was a Sunni, his mother a Shiite. He had converted to his mother's sect years earlier and joined Hezbollah. His family wanted him buried in a Sunni cemetery. But the Sunni hard-liners would not have him. The entrance to the cemetery was blocked by protesters. "His body should be thrown into the sea," one protester said. The army sent a unit to separate the feuding sides. Hezbollah settled the matter: the fighter was buried in a Shia cemetery. The place was beyond mixed marriages and divided identities. Men like Hassan Nasrallah and Ahmad al-Assir had run away with their communities.

Offended and provoked by Hezbollah, the Sunni jihad found a perfect setting: Tripoli, Lebanon's second-largest city. Unlike Sidon, Tripoli was at a great physical remove from the Shia territories. Devoutly Sunni, insular in its outlook, and suspicious of Beirut, Tripoli had never wanted to be part of Lebanon to begin with. Its economy and social and religious life were extensions of Homs. A thriving port city, Tripoli looked to the Syrian interior and aspired to a role as Syria's principal trading center. The city had to be forced into the Lebanese polity that the French had put together in the 1920s. There would be no peace for Tripoli in the Lebanese republic. The civic religion of the city was Arab nationalism, anchored in a conservative Muslim sensibility.

The Syrian rebellion was bound to pull in Tripoli. Syrian Sunnis, in such close proximity, were being assaulted by Alawi schismatics, and Tripoli's mosques and jihadist networks were quick to take up their brethren's cause. To make matters worse, Tripoli had an Alawi minority of its own that had ridden the coattails of the Syrian regime during its long occupation of Lebanon. The lines were drawn in this city: there was an Alawi neighborhood, Jabal Mohsen, that faced a Sunni neighborhood, Bab al-Tabbaneh. The two neighborhoods were divided by Syria Street! If the French had forced Tripoli into Lebanon, this war, nearly a century later, was testing Tripoli's fidelity. There was a particularly fierce animus toward Hezbollah. Tripoli's jihadists were hunted down by the Lebanese army, while Hezbollah's warriors were beyond the reach of the authorities. Wealth and resentment mattered as well. Tripoli was an orphan, while Hezbollah's Iranian patronage and extortion rackets gave it considerable wealth and resources.

V: A WAR WITH NO VICTORS

After a siege of three weeks, Qusayr fell to the combined forces of the regime and Hezbollah on June 5, 2013. In the Shia suburbs of southern Beirut there was glee and celebration. Sweets were handed to passers-by, and banners proclaimed the fall of Qusayr. On June 8, there came footage from Qusayr that was sectarian in the extreme. In the images from the doomed town, masked Hezbollah fighters are celebrating to martial music and holding up a black banner reading "O Hussein," which they place atop the minaret of a town mosque. It so happened that the Sunni mosque is named after the second of the four Rightly Guided Caliphs, Umar ibn al-Khattab. Umar is anathema to the Shia; in the Shia narrative, he had usurped Imam Ali's right to the caliphate and triumphed while Ali had suffered the pain of disinheritance. An old account with Umar was being settled in that broken, defeated town. Qusayr was declared a "Shia city"; its conquerors had traveled far beyond their insistence on their own virtue and clean hands.

Hezbollah was leading the Shia of Lebanon away from their truths and necessities of their fragile country, away from the caution that Arab Shiism had long counseled for its adherents.

The protagonists were not done. After Qusayr, trouble came directly to Sidon. The Syrian regime had begun calling for settling matters in Sidon and cleansing it of *takfiri* (denouncing someone as a *kafir*, an unbeliever) elements. The regime sought a battle with Ahmad al-Assir and his band of armed men. Typical of Nasrallah, he now spoke the language of order: *takfiris* could not roam free in Sidon, and mosques would not be permitted to become storehouses for weapons. Nasrallah had a powerful weapon at his disposal: the Lebanese state that he had subverted to his purposes and the national army whose commanders were accomplices of Hezbollah. Assir was no tactician, and he was badly outmatched. Less than three weeks after the fall of Qusayr, he entered a battle he could not win with army units stationed in Sidon. In the first round, 10 soldiers had been killed. The Sidon bourgeoisie now wanted to be done with Assir.

He made a run for it, and it was rumored that he did not let his men in on his escape. It was said that he sought shelter in the Palestinian refugee camps on Sidon's outskirts. There were other reports that he made his way to a safer Sunni stronghold—Tripoli.

Sidon had looked into the abyss, and its establishment wanted to pull back. In a Friday sermon, on June 28, the Mufti of Sidon, the designated head of the Sunni religious institution, walked a narrow plank. He expressed sympathy and offered condolences for the fallen soldiers as he gave voice to his community's grievances. The army is a guarantee of social peace, he said, but some "elements within it" had damaged the image and reputation of the military institution. It was unacceptable for extralegal armed units to arrest people and interrogate them. "We don't accept that people are led to prison because they are bearded or donning veils. The state is responsible for the maintenance of order; without its protection people will lose faith and deviate from the straight path." Thus spoke the voice of caution. But the mufti did not have the occasion to himself. As he spoke, followers of Ahmad al-Assir chanted his name and wanted nothing to do with offering condolences to the "martyrs" of the army.

The Sunni Arab order of power—the rulers, the merchants, the bureaucrats, and the military officers—had not been blameless. The Sunni gate-keepers in Beirut had not been eager to welcome the Shia squatters and urban migrants as they made their way from the Bekaa Valley and the southern hinterland. The political order of Beirut, and of the Lebanese republic as a whole, rested on an accommodation between the Maronites and the Sunnis. The Shia were an afterthought, peasants trying to scrub themselves clean from their past. The lords of Sunni Beirut were scions of old bourgeois families—lawyers and merchants, judges and state functionaries. In their better days they had sprawling houses with gardens and knew the ease of what was still an intimate city. When they stepped out of their community, they forged bonds with their peers in the city, the Greek Orthodox notables, city folks with polish and skills. The Sunni "street" was pan-Arabist in outlook, and it never really bothered with the Shia; the latter were the unwashed stepchildren.

Beyond the confines of Lebanon, the Sunnis had wider Arab horizons. They could find political patrons in Egypt, the Arabian Peninsula, or Baghdad. Their world was bigger than that of the insular Shia world digging out of poverty and marginality. The change in fortunes in the 1980s, which had seen the rise of the Shia, was, to the Sunnis, a violation of the proper order of things. The "street" toughs who could defend Sunni West Beirut were swept aside. In the 1970s, the protection of the Sunnis had passed to the Palestinian militias—fellow Sunnis invested in keeping the turf they had carved out in Lebanon. The eviction of the Palestinian organizations from Lebanon by Israel in the war of 1982 signaled the end of Sunni dominion—the praetorian guard had left. Israel had done for the Shia what they had not been able to do for themselves. The Sunni urban notables had been living on borrowed time. When Yasser Arafat and the fighters of the Palestine Liberation

Organization boarded the ships that would take them to their new sanctuary in faraway Tunisia, an era had ended. The Shia were now free to make their own history, with all its warts—and satisfactions.

VI: A FOREIGNER'S GIFT: LIBERATION IN IRAQ

In Iraq, the Shia had lived through their own history of humiliation and defeat. There was a Sunni expression that provided a fair reflection of the standing of the Shia: *Lanna al hukum wa lakkum al-latm* (We have the dominion and you have the self-flagellation). In his 2005 book, *Al-Iraq al-Amriki (American Iraq),* Hassan al-Alawi, a sophisticated diplomat, had accurately described the two groups as the sect of the rulers and the sect of the ruled. The ascendency of the Sunnis in the Ottoman provinces had been a natural fact of life. The modern Iraqi state that the British had built in 1921 had simply codified that dominion. A big revolt had broken out in the middle Euphrates in the south of Iraq against the British in 1920. This eruption would become legendary, but its harvest was the destruction of Shia power and Anglo-Sunni rule over the new kingdom. Out of the rebellion, the British occupation emerged with an aversion to the Shia "divines" in Najaf and Kerbala and a suspicion of their links to Persia. Hassan al-Alawi described the outcome of this revolt in stark terms: the Sunnis got a political kingdom, while the Shia were left with the "rusty, old rifles" of the Marsh Arabs and the tales of heroism.

In the new Hashemite kingdom that the British had midwifed, pride of place went to a political class of ex-Ottomanist officers and bureaucrats who rode the coattails of the British and accompanied the Hashemite prince, King Faisal I, into a kingdom he had never set foot in before. An uncompromising doctrine of Arab nationalism was the perfect ideology for a ruling elite estranged from the Shia tribal notables and seminarians and from the Kurds. There would be no happiness in this new realm—King Faisal I was a decent and prudent man, but he despaired of the new century and its feuds. He bore the Shia no animus. But it was different with the men who claimed and hoarded power in this new country.

The holy Shia cities of Najaf and Kerbala were loathed by this bureaucratic elite, as were the Shia rituals of grief and lamentations. In the cruelest of ironies, the ex-Ottomanist rulers "Persianized" the Shia of Iraq, writing them off as a tributary of the Persian state next door.

The Shia, with a few exceptions, quit the political realm and turned to commerce. They were to fill the void left by the expulsion of Iraqi Jews in 1950–51. But the state would eventually come into dominion of the market, and the Shia merchants would be stripped of their leadership of the chambers of commerce in Baghdad and Basra. The fall of the monarchy in 1958 would pose new dilemmas for the Shia. The military officers who would dominate the new realm were men of Tikrit and Fallujah, Baquba and Mosul. They were mainly men of the poorer strata, alienated from the Shia merchants of Baghdad. With oil money, state terror, and the exalted claims of Arab nationalism, they left little room for the Shia. In time, the whirlwind of Iraqi politics would bring to the fore a despot bereft of mercy and subtlety, Saddam Hussein. He offered the Shia seminarians and their leaders, and the Marsh Arabs in the south, the option of servitude and quietism. He would deport at will to Iran thousands who had known no other home than Iraq. He imposed a reign of terror in Najaf and Kerbala. In a searing episode in 1980, his regime executed a Shia cleric of noble descent, Ayatollah Muhammad Baqir al-Sadr, along with the cleric's sister, Bint al-Huda, an accomplished poet and thinker. Saddam closed up the political universe in Iraq. But in a variation on the quintessential theme of Shia dispossession and sudden redemption, the Tikriti despot ran afoul of a mighty power looking to avenge the terror inflicted on it by a band of Arab death pilots. The United States was in no mood for fine distinctions between Arabs guilty of those hideous attacks and others who had winked at the terror. Saddam drew the short straw, as it were. The United States had not struck Iraq to empower the Shia and rid them of the Sunni ascendency. But history had its own cunning. Baghdad, the seat of the Abbasid caliphate, would come under Shia rule. The Sunni Arab states recoiled at this outcome, but they could not reverse it.

VII: THE MATTER OF STATE POWER

State power has always been *ghanima* (spoils of war) in these lands. Lucky were the ones who acquired it or were bequeathed it by outsiders. A mix of group effort and foreign patronage has dictated the outcome of these contests. Lebanon must be reckoned the least deadly of these contests. The country never had a powerful state to begin with; its principal communities thrived on their own. In addition to their philanthropies, educational institutions, and civic associations, they had their own "muscle." The first national compact was drawn in the 1940s, and it invested primacy in the two most resourceful sects: the Christian Maronites and the Sunnis. This arrangement held until the mid–1980s, when history broke the way of the Shia. Had the Shia remained the Lebanonists of old, their rise and newfound power would have been true to the country's history. But Hezbollah was not a local phenomenon—it didn't live off the land, and it didn't play by the local rules. The power Iran made available to Hezbollah would, in time, overwhelm the country's delicate balance. A nation-state whose standing army was weaker than the dominant militia had little claim on legitimacy and power. The Hezbollah fighters parading with their banners and heavy weapons, with their salaries and welfare needs provided by the Iranian theocracy, were not truly citizens of Lebanon.

It is hard to see Hezbollah holding on to the power it had come to accumulate. The myth of the "resistance" against Israel that gave Hezbollah its raison d'être has been spent. Outside the Hezbollah believers, no one has for Hassan Nasrallah and his oratory the indulgence extended in earlier years. The Lebanese have wearied of him and his subservience to Tehran. The guns will still give Hezbollah a place, as will the weight of Shia demography and resources. But there are only so many wars on the Israeli-Lebanese border that the people of Lebanon, and the Shia, can bear in silence. Hezbollah has placed the Shia of Lebanon on a collision course with the Sunni Arab states. This is not a workable proposition for a people who live on the commerce and hospitality of strangers. Already the

Arab states of the Persian Gulf have begun to make it much harder for Lebanese Shia to find or keep coveted jobs and business opportunities. One way or the other, the Lebanese will want the restoration of balance in their country. They will grant Hezbollah its share of power and no more. The Shia were once Lebanon's hewers of wood and drawers of water. That lies behind them. But Hezbollah can't rule Lebanon alone. The guns and missiles of Hezbollah could still land Lebanon into a war with Israel, with terrible consequences for all.

It is a matter of no small irony that Lebanon, the merchant republic on the Mediterranean, had been turned into a fortress regime for Iran and its local satrap. Lebanon had a founding father, a banker—of all professions—by the name of Michel Chiha (1891–1954). Chiha was a Greek Catholic pragmatist who saw Lebanon as a "Mediterranean country" of trade and services, an heir to the great Phoenician cities. For Chiha, the Lebanese were to be "friends of the masters of the world," artisans, and traders. "We are a place where men acclimatize themselves wherever they come from, where civilizations meet, where beliefs, languages, and liturgies bow to each other; a Mediterranean country first and foremost but like the Mediterranean itself, sensitive to every man's poetry."

Lebanese journalist Mohamed Abi Samra recalled Chiha's legacy in a November 22, 2013, article in *An Nahar,* aptly titled "From Michel Chiha's Lebanon to the Lebanon of Hassan Nasrallah." According to Abi Samra, the country has been altered beyond recognition, its mission subverted. Instead of the banker and pragmatist of old, there is now a turbaned warrior in a bunker deciding matters of war and peace.

The powers of the world have wearied of Lebanon. For all practical purposes, the country was written off in the mid-1980s, when the United States packed up its gear and left after a frustrating effort to give the country a chance. The last memory, a searing image, Americans had of Beirut was the October 23, 1983, attack on the US Marine barracks by the Beirut airport. A young boy drove a Mercedes-Benz truck loaded with TNT through the barricades, killing 241 US servicemen. American missionaries and educators had known the city since the

1820s; they had savored it and stamped it with their ways. Now Beirut was claimed by darkness and ruin. Damascus and Tehran were content to fill the void. These two regimes had no scruples and no mercy. There was a fleeting moment of hope for the Lebanese in the spring of 2005, when the Cedar Revolution ignited dreams of a sovereign, independent country. But with Hezbollah on the ground, there was to be no exit for Lebanon from the politics of murder and mayhem.

It will be much harder for the ruling Alawis in Syria to find a "normal" world. They grabbed power by the gun, and the Sunni quiescence that made it possible is gone for good. Alawi rule was always a historical anomaly. It lacked the weight of numbers in the face of a Sunni majority, and it never had the "social capital" that the Maronite primacy had in Lebanon— the education and the skills that helped reconcile the other communities of the country at the ascendency of the Maronites. None of this obtained in Syria with the Alawis. In an old urban civilization the rule of peasant soldiers was unnatural. It was enforced with the whip and the intelligence services, but it was resented all the more because the men in power were uncouth soldiers who hailed from an esoteric sect.

The Assad dictatorship may ride out this crisis, and it may or may not hold on to Damascus. There is, of course, speculation that the Alawis may make a run for their mountain abode by the coast. The violence inflicted by the regime is unlikely to be forgiven. A different cabal from the Alawi community will have to negotiate the terms of a new compact with the Sunni majority. They needn't be angels; at a minimum, they will have to be able to claim a measure of innocence from the slaughter. It will be very different for the Alawis once they are shorn of their monopoly on state power. Gone is the ability of the Alawi regime to extort protection money from the wealthy Arab state in the name of a "sacred" fight with Israel. The Sunni Arabs are done with the Alawis. If an Alawi statelet is to make a stand, it will have to rely on the largesse of a Russia eager to claim, and pay for, a base of power in the Mediterranean.

It was said of Old Man Assad that he was Syria's Josip Broz Tito. Tito had held Yugoslavia together by guile and force, and after his death all the suppressed nationalisms came to the fore. Hafez al-Assad may have been that kind of historical figure for Syria. He gave it three decades of stability—and fear. He built his regime on the group solidarity of the Alawis, the quiescence of the Sunni *ulama*, and the willingness of the Sunni merchant class to leave politics to the military. His regime had been a beneficiary of the advantages the French rulers of interwar Syria had given the Alawis. That republic has been undone, and in the wreckage can be seen Syria's true fragments: the Alawi mountain coast, the Kurds in the northeast, the Druze in their mountainous country in the southeast, and a Sunni majority that awakened to its rights and to no small measure of guilt as to its own quiescence.

Syrians once lived on the legend that their country was the "beating heart of Arabism." Successive regimes convinced the Syrians that their country had a mission, and they took on Israel and American power as well. The fighter planes of the regime's air force pounding Aleppo and the desperate parents taking their wounded children, in silence, to Israeli hospitals ought to bring such fraudulent claims to a long-overdue end.

On paper, Iraq has the potential for a workable national compact. To begin with, the Shia are the majority and the Sunnis know their campaign has been fought and lost. The treasury of the state, due to its vast oil reserves, can be deployed with skill and generosity to calm the tempest in the Sunni stronghold of western Iraq. Blood has been shed in Iraq, to be sure, but the rancid hate that separates the Alawis and the Sunnis of Syria is alien to Iraq. Many tribes in Iraq have Sunni and Shia "branches," and a ruler more skillful than the one the country has been afflicted with in recent years can see his way to a national compact. The Sunni ascendency—think of it as an Ottoman-British gift—has been toppled by an American war and by Shia demography. For their part, the Shia, after the heady acquisition of power, will have to accept the burdens and the limitations that come with newfound power.

In truth, Iraq has always been a disappointment. It had vast oil reserves, abundant water,

agricultural land, and a sophisticated profes-
sional class. The British who, in their heady
moments, invented Iraq thought it would serve
as a model for other Arab states to follow.
Gertrude Bell, the "kingmaker" of the Hashemite order (1921–1958), once spoke unabashedly
of her protégé, Faisal I, ruling the region from
Mesopotamia to the Mediterranean. The Arab
Nationalists picked it as the Prussia of their
imagination, the country that would unite the
Arabs and keep the Persians at bay. Those who
spoke of Iraq as the "eastern gateway" of the
Arab world endowed it with that mission. And,
truth be told, the Americans, too, in their brief
regency after 2003 entertained ideas of a big
regional role for Iraq, a balance to Iran, and per-
haps an alternative to Saudi Arabia—less xeno-
phobic, more open to American influence.

But the Iraq to emerge from the American
stewardship has gone its own way. Nuri Kamal
al-Maliki's Iraq—and one can speak of it thusly—
turned out to be a sectarian and a personal tyr-
anny. Maliki was not particularly impressive,
but the Shia heartland took to him. The hope
that Baghdad would balance Tehran was set

aside as Maliki sought patronage in Iran against his rivals in the Shia political class. I am reminded of a young Iraqi who was, effectively, my tutor as I tried to make sense of the country for a book I was writing after the American invasion. "Iraq is a graveyard for all dreams," he said. The remark was sweeping. It took in British, Arab, Iranian, and American dreams. After the ordeal of Iraq in 2013—more than 8,000 Iraqis killed in the violence of that year—one can be forgiven the thought that a fatal brand haunts that country. Statehood remains elusive. Some dark thoughts about Iraq were penned by King Faisal I shortly before his death in 1933. These retain their power and merit quoting at length.

"In Iraq there is still—and I say this with a heart full of sorrow—no Iraqi people but unimaginable masses of human beings, devoid of any patriotic idea, imbued with religious traditions and absurdities, connected by no common tie, giving ear to evil, prone to anarchy, and perpetually ready to rise against any government whatever. Out of these masses we want to fashion a people which we would train, educate, and refine. . . . The circumstances, being what they are, the immenseness of the efforts needed for this [can be imagined]."

There is one national community in Iraq that has made the best of what the American war made possible: the Kurds. Over the past decade, Iraqi Kurdistan has erected the foundations of a decent polity. There was no need to declare independence from Iraq as the facts on the ground spoke for themselves. There was effective governance in Kurdistan as the rest of Iraq was consumed with violence. Oil revenue brought prosperity to Kurdistan, and Erbil, the capital city, had emerged as a serious player in the region's politics. Like a phoenix, Kurdistan has risen out of the ashes of a tormented history. Kurds beyond Iraq have taken notice. The Syrian Kurds, in particular, can do well for themselves emulating the pragmatism of their brethren in Iraq.

The fractures of Lebanon, Syria, and Iraq being what they are, there will always be a role for outside powers. Of the three powers competing for influence, Saudi Arabia and Iran are in it for the long haul. Each of these powers has a sense of mission and constituencies that enable them to stick it out and pay the price for a sphere of influence. It is hard to see Iran bidding farewell to the power it accumulated in Iraq, Syria, and Lebanon. Iran is good at leveraging its power in these contested places. In the same vein, the Saudis see themselves as protectors of the Sunni communities in these three countries. That leaves Turkey; the "Sunnification" of its foreign policy is less convincing. Prime Minister Recep Tayyip Erdogan has not fully enlisted his country in his drive into Arab affairs. As the burdens of the Syrian war mounted, so did the pressure in Turkey to walk away from the complications.

There was the burden of the Syrian refugees to begin with, and the vast majority of them had sought shelter in the Hatay province by the border with Syria, an area with a tangled demography and a sizeable Alawi community that had remained when Turkey annexed the province in 1939. With the refugees came deeds of terror. On May 11, 2013, two car bombs exploded in the town of Reyhanli, killing 51 people. This was

Turkey's most deadly deed of terror. Car bombs were routine in Damascus, Beirut, and Baghdad, but not so in Turkey. The Turks never bargained for so costly an Arab expedition. They had expected a quick end for the Assad regime, and they were convinced that the American cavalry would ride to the rescue and settle the fight for Syria to Turkey's advantage. The disinterest shown by the Obama administration was a great surprise for the Turks. Before long, there would be growing pressure in Turkey to leave Syria—and the Arabs—to their own troubles.

VIII: THE LAST REFUGE?

It would be tempting to argue that Iran had run away with Shiism and that the faith had been Persianized. After all, Iran is the only Shia state in the world of Islam. Its demography and weight in the diplomatic councils, not to mention the very audacity of its bid for power, grant it influence that appears to overwhelm the other centers of Shiism. But that temptation ought to be resisted. Iran's doctrinal notion of *wilayat al-faqih* is an overreach; it makes no allowance for nationalism, and it superimposes the needs of a clerical regime in Tehran over those of the Shia of Iraq, Lebanon, the Arab states of the Gulf, etc. Shia clerics and laymen at some remove from Iran can't be bullied into submission.

This tension between Iran's brand of the faith and that of other centers of Shiism can be traced to the very different ways Shiism spread in Arab lands and the manner in which it came to Iran in the sixteenth century. For all of Iran's influence, there are profound differences between the "organic" growth of Shiism in its habitat and the imposition of Shiism as practically a state religion by the Safavids in the opening years of the sixteenth century. Imperial competition between the Sunni Ottoman state and the Persian state next door was the impetus behind the imposition of Shiism from above. Religious scholars had to be brought into Iran from Iraq, Bahrain, and the Shia country in Jabal Amil in south Lebanon. Iran was bigger and wealthier, and an ambitious mullah could see the possibilities of a better life in the new Shia domain. A faith that enjoyed state patronage in Iran could not possess the same temperament as variants of it that took hold among men on the run, persecuted by the rulers and hounded by Sunni religious scholars.

In this vein two decades ago, an eminent Shia scholar with roots in Iraq and Lebanon, Ayatollah Mohammad Hussein Fadlallah (1935–2010), sought to build in the Shia neighborhoods of Beirut an alternative to Iran's interpretation and of Shiism. Fadlallah was an accomplished poet with a keen sense of the politics of Lebanon. He had lived and worked among the Shia of northeast Beirut and alongside the Armenians. He had followers and financial backers among the Shia elite. He and the leaders of Hezbollah kept a discreet distance from each other. Iran's notion of *wilayat al-faqih,* he openly stated, could not survive on Lebanese soil. It was a leap into the void, he said, in a small country of diverse religious communities. Fadlallah never did bend to Iran's will. He had faith in his own scholarship; he had been educated in Najaf, where he spent his early years, and was not above baiting Iran's scholars on their mastery of the (Arabic) sources of Shiism. Fadlallah savored Beirut and thought he would establish an alternative to Iranian dogma in that freewheeling city.

Sayyid Muhammad Reda al-Ghurayfi, a revered man of the clerical estate and the overseer of the shrine of Imam Ali in Najaf, some years ago reminded me that politics does not sweep all in its way. "We have nothing to do with Iran," he said to me. "We share the same faith, but we are different. We don't want Iran to rule us. Najaf is the sun. It transcends all, and all the other cities of the Shia world revolve around it, live off its illumination." Ghurayfi had power and influence. He was Grand Ayatollah Ali al-Sistani's trusted aide, and the Shia men in power in Baghdad sought his company and blessing. But, still, the Shia tradition of centuries at the receiving end of power and persecution tugged at him. "For fourteen centuries, no ruler has given us justice, but we have endured. But above all we are repelled by the shedding of blood, because our blood was shed for so long and by so many. The Shia of Imam Ali are born to suffering. We have to be in a constant state of agitation. The agitation made us what we are. We are born oppositionists."

Ghurayfi related to me an episode he savored. Hezbollah leader Hassan Nasrallah had sent an envoy to Najaf to repair a breach that had opened between the militia in Beirut and the holy city in Iraq. The envoy was sent home empty-handed. "We told him to go back and tell his leader that we are constantly praying for his undoing. We are through with the likes of Nasrallah."

For those long centuries that Ghurayfi invoked, Shiism outwitted its tormentors. It would be a singular tale of loss and sorrow if Hezbollah, Iran's Revolutionary Guard, and the newly empowered Shia warlords in Iraq, were to sully Shiism with their dark deeds, taking away from it the sense of mercy that was always its guiding light.

SOURCE NOTES

On men jumbling the past and future, see Hannah Arendt's *Between Past and Future,* Viking Press, New York (1961).

Readers interested in the political culture of the Shia of Lebanon, see Fouad Ajami's *The Vanished Imam: Musa al Sadr and the Shia of Lebanon,* Cornell University Press, 1992.

For further reading on Hafez al-Assad and Bashar al-Assad's relationship with Iran, consult Itamar Rabinovich's *The View from Damascus: State, Political Community and Foreign Relations in Twentieth Century Syria,* Vallentine Mitchell, 2008.

For an authoritative source on Iraqi Shiites, see Yitzhak Nakash's seminal book, *The Shi'is of Iraq,* Princeton University Press, 2000.

Hassan al-Alawi, in his book *Al-Iraq al-Amriki (American Iraq),* London, 2005, describes the two sects in Iraq—the rulers and the ruled.

ABOUT THE AUTHOR

FOUAD AJAMI is the Herbert and Jane Dwight Senior Fellow at the Hoover Institution and the cochair of the Herbert and Jane Dwight Working Group on Islamism and the International Order. From 1980 to 2011 he was professor and director of Middle East Studies at The Johns Hopkins School of Advanced International Studies. He is the author of *The Arab Predicament, The Vanished Imam: Musa al Sadr and the Shia of Lebanon, Beirut: City of Regrets, The Dream Palace of the Arabs,* and *The Foreigner's Gift: The Americans, the Arabs, and the Iraqis in Iraq.* His most recent book is *The Syrian Rebellion* (Hoover Institution Press, 2012). He is a widely published essayist whose writings, reviews and columns of opinion, have appeared in *Foreign Affairs, The New Republic, The Wall Street Journal, The New*

York Times Book Review, Foreign Policy, The New York Times Magazine, and other forums in the United States and abroad.

Ajami is the recipient of the five-year MacArthur Prize Fellowship, which he was awarded in 1982. In 2006, he was granted the Bradley Prize for Outstanding Achievement. In November 2006, he was awarded the National Humanities Medal by the President of the United States. In June 2011, he was awarded The Eric Breindel Prize for Excellence in Opinion Journalism. In November 2011, he received the seventh annual Benjamin Franklin Public Service Award from the Foreign Policy Research Institute in Philadelphia. His research has charted the road to 9/11, the Iraq war, and the US presence in the Arab-Islamic world.

HERBERT AND JANE DWIGHT
WORKING GROUP ON
ISLAMISM AND THE
INTERNATIONAL ORDER

THE HERBERT AND JANE DWIGHT WORKING
GROUP ON ISLAMISM AND THE INTERNATIONAL
ORDER seeks to engage in the task of reversing Islamic radicalism through reforming and strengthening the legitimate role of the state across the entire Muslim world. Efforts will draw on the intellectual resources of an array of scholars and practitioners from within the United States and abroad, to foster the pursuit of modernity, human flourishing, and the rule of law and reason in Islamic lands—developments that are critical to the very order of the international system.

The Working Group is cochaired by Hoover fellows Fouad Ajami and Charles Hill, with an active participation by Hoover Institution Director John Raisian. Current core membership includes Russell A. Berman and Abbas Milani, with contributions from Zeyno Baran, Marius Deeb, Reuel Marc Gerecht, Ziad Haider, R. John Hughes, Nibras Kazimi, Bernard Lewis, Habib C. Malik, Camille Pecastaing, Itamar Rabinovich, Lieutenant Colonel Joel Rayburn, Lee Smith, Samuel Tadros, Joshua Teitelbaum, and Tunku Varadarajan.

Freedom or Terror: Europe Faces Jihad
Russell A. Berman

The Myth of the Great Satan:
A New Look at America's Relations with Iran
Abbas Milani

Torn Country: Turkey between Secularism and Islamism
Zeyno Baran

Islamic Extremism and the War of Ideas: Lessons from Indonesia
R. John Hughes

The End of Modern History in the Middle East
Bernard Lewis

The Wave: Man, God, and the Ballot Box in the Middle East
Reuel Marc Gerecht

Trial of a Thousand Years: World Order and Islamism
Charles Hill

Jihad in the Arabian Sea
Camille Pecastaing

The Syrian Rebellion
Fouad Ajami

Motherland Lost: The Egyptian and Coptic Quest for Modernity
Samuel Tadros

Iraq after America: Strongmen, Sectarians, Resistance
Joel Rayburn

[For a list of essays published under the auspices of the
WORKING GROUP ON ISLAMISM AND THE INTERNATIONAL ORDER,
please see page ii.]

INDEX